Disclaimer: Due to the content of the material, this book is intended for mature audiences only.

A TASTE OF HONIE

STACEY BARLOW

A Taste Of Honie

By: Stacey Barlow

Cover Art by Darlene Annette Taylor
Created by Jazzy Kitty Publications
Logo Designs by Andre M. Saunders/Leroy Grayson
Editor: Stacey Barlow
Co-editor: Anelda Attaway

© 2020 Stacey Barlow
ISBN 978-1-7349014-4-3
Library of Congress Control Number: 2020910208

All rights reserved. This book is protected by the copyright laws of the United States of America. This book may not be copied or reprinted for commercial gain or profit. The use of short quotations or occasional page copying for personal or group study is permitted and encouraged. Permission will be granted upon request. For Worldwide Distribution. Printed in the United States of America. Published by Jazzy Kitty Publications utilizing Microsoft Publishing Software and Bookcover Pro. The Holy Scriptures are from the Holy Bible.

ACKNOWLEDGMENTS

Giving Honor and Glory to my Heavenly Father for giving me this gift and allowing me share it with the world. There is no better way to express the love that has been given from you ~ Thank you.

To my family for all the love and support that you have given me down through the years; I don't know what I'd do without you.

To my friends which are too many to name and my very special muse Miss Latoya "Miss Toya The Poetess" Jackson Williams; if it wasn't for you, I would have stopped using my gift that was given ~ I thank you.

To Anabelle Muños Cotto for your assisting me with the poem Mojito ~ you are appreciated.

To Mrs. Anelda Attaway, my publisher for blessing me to share my art with the world. I only pray that because of your undying love for the art that you will continue to be blessed and bless others by helping them ~ I thank you from within.

My Rocks: Juanita Barlow, Sarah Henderson, DeAna A Smith, Rene Daniels, Kiana Smith, Darlene Annette Taylor, Kathy Vaughn, Gina Haggard Couch, Chella Johnson and the late Angela Perry (you will always be my rock ~ I love you ~ and deep in my heart ~ April 24, 1967-December 5, 2011).

Lucky 7 ~ I can't say enough. . .your words have stayed with me for many years. I love you ~ Thank you. Stacey~

DEDICATIONS

To the late Angela Perry {April 24, 1967-December 5, 2011}. We have grown up together, sung together, rolled together, laughed, and cried together. Although it has been a while, I still find it difficult to let you go but, I know God saw it fit to take you home to be with Him. You stood by me when I needed a shoulder and prayer; and assured me that we all go through the same things but, each of us handle things differently. My dear sweet cousin, you are truly an angel and will always be my ace.

To the late Dennis Frazier {September 5, 1958-October 21, 2018} You were my hero and my rock on earth. I appreciate your friendship even through our rough times. The most beautiful thing about a loving heart is that it's always open to give. I loved our time together. You made me feel like I can do anything above normal. You were my Batman. There will never be anyone else like you. Thank you for the encouragement throughout the years. I love you with everything in me.

TABLE OF CONTENTS

Introduction	i
70's Love Grove	01
About That Life	04
Back In The Day	06
Boomerang Effect	07
Breathe (Where Is He?)	13
Bullisht Talk (Telephone Drop Late Night Call)	16
Buried Treasure (A Plea To Be Found)	22
Can I Rock Witchu?	24
Can't Sleep	26
Challenge My Heart	27
Cipher (A Kwansaba)	30
Circle (My Dilemma)	31
Cream	34
Emperor's Ways	37
Face Me (Quiet Storm Trilogy For "You")	40
Four Chambers	44
Frequency	46
From Grave To Gravesite	48
G.A.M.E. (Giving All My Energy)	51
Get Pass This	56
Have You Given Thanks Today?	58

TABLE OF CONTENTS

He Made Me Cry 60

Head Piece (Fantasy Of Mr. Big) 62

I Need A Pen To My Pad 65

I Want Your… 70

If I Were His (Daydreaming) 74

In The Meantime 76

Indescribably Amazing 79

Infinity 82

Invisible 83

Kutabare (Devil's F*ckery) 84

Last First Kiss 86

Let's Play (Me, Her and Him) 90

Little Laura (Wood) 93

May I Try Again Tonight? 96

Mirror 100

My Casualty 103

My Everything (You Are) 107

My Everything (The Rejection) 109

My Lover 114

My Mojito 117

New Sheriff In Town 119

No More Footprints (2:15 a.m.) 121

TABLE OF CONTENTS

Open To Give 124
Quality Fabric Of A Man.. 126
Rain Dance 131
Rise Above (Hurricane Mix for "Him") 133
Secrets (Before You Go ~ Collaboration w/Shadowstep) 137
Shadow Dancing (Step Into My Dream) 142
Shadow Run.. 145
Stand Still... 148
Take It To The Head (Stop Running) 150
Tastes Great 154
The Elevator 157
Tick Tick Boom (WOOOSAAAAH Moment) 160
Twin Flames 163
Who (Else) Is Loving You?... 166
Wholeheartedly (Reaching Out) 171
Heaven Doesn't Have To Wait 173
About the Author 176

INTRODUCTION

Let's play a little game of whose heart gets broken first. From the love of one to the love of many, all hearts are involved. In true form, love can be beautiful, love can be harsh, love can become lonesome and unforgiving. The journey through one's heart is a very long one and time-consuming. Will you have the time to travel and feel what others may feel?

Love is never boastful or prideful. Love should be one on one, one at a time, and not a lot of people at once. You may want to get on that merry go round of confusion and get off at what you may think is a safe stop and find yourself dealing with being in the dark about love. There are many relationships among men and women, women and women, men and men. A few are not condoned but love is love and you cannot help who you love.

This magical ride is not for the faint of heart but, for those who have gone through the struggle of trying to keep a love and keep a relationship spicy. There is a dark side to love especially when a heart has been broken. The thoughts of the other person can become sinister, and usually, there is no turning back from it. Time to go to the other side of a heart that is broken. Can it be mended? It's up to the people involved. Let the *insider* tell the story of love, lust, heartbreak, and mind death from the alter ego point of view. What's true? What's fiction?

It's time to come out on the other side.

70's Love Groove

Chakra stones under my pillow
healing stones under my feet
bullet, rabbit, vibrator and
Big Boi to feel some heat
I feel so broken hearted with
what I just read
hanging beads
hot candle wax
incense burning
getting ready for my bed
partner in tow all stretched
preparing for a
midnight rendezvous
blindfolded by nature
and choice of being tied too
what ever is need needed
me, my body and YOU
lights flickering against
the walls as our bodies
dance
one position, two position

three position. . .four

we got the foreplay out of the way

now it's time for romance

rising above to make it seem

like I want my

back broken

to the left to the right

in the middle

dig deeper to the bottom

to get your gold token

sweat dripping to the tip of my

nose

you got my thighs all soaking wet

and that's the way the story

goes

you told the fellows

you broke my back

in five different places

I told my girls

I broke yours in six

in spaces

You can't move because

I don't want you to

I took the blindfold off and untied

You

three hours in and I'm

not done yet

I did say me

not you

I need to

burn to get wet

spotlight

and the shadows are dancing

it's all in the

70's love groove

I need more love

than romancing

About That Life

Loving a man who says he's

"about that life"

But "about that life"

Can lead him to the new life that he's so desiring to

Capture "about that life"

Which won't ever lead him back to that life

Granted that he's "all about that life"

Found a love who is "all about that life"

To

Change his life by

Being

Nice

About her life

Which may rub off on his life

Being "about that life"

That he may crave no more

But still have life in him

To give her life back in

A different form

Effecting her old life to become

A part of his new life

Together

On some real life

Changing his whole world to become

Her world and letting

Him know

She's **"about that life"** that

He really wants

And in the end

They are both loving the life

So they can tell their story

"about that life"

More gas no breaks

Back in the Day

At the crack of dawn

at the age of five

spending the summer with my aunt Hazel

in Galveston TX...

why does everybody seem to go there?

share a laugh

with cooked breakfast, lunch and dinner

being chased by the neighborhood kids

because

they didn't like me

partying with my cousins

late into the midnight hour

going to bed

as I stared at the street light

I knew I would be a star

My aunt is no longer here

with me

Boomerang Effect

Are we ready to begin

again?

let you and I

start at the beginning

let me take you

back

back

Back

to the times where

we had the most fun

and then made love

Are we ready?

I can throw at you

anything that won't frighten

you

And you can throw back

at me

things that

won't have me

second guessing

things you

do

Losing sleep while

you sit, wait

and run

through my

R.E.M.

My brain

throws my

intellect into high

gear

Like that Casablanca

film

I love this man

like the stars need

the sky and

the river

needs

the moon

really don't want

to be turned around

and thrown

back again

too soon

I love this man

like a flower

needs

water

and a bee

needs its

nectar

you got me feeling ill

will

with this

boomerang effect

OR

is it that I'm

still trippin'

Over the

love we

made

that's got my head

spinning round and round

like a rollercoaster?

Are you ready

to begin again

so that I can

have it

be

it is what

it is

or what I think

it is

it will be

get me?

I love this man

like

paper to pencil

and ink

to pen

this man is

my poetry in

motion

my soul surviving

entity

my deep within

are you ready

to

spread your wings

and receive the love

that needs to

be giving back

to you?

Or are you detonating

that boomerang

effect

to not receive the love

that's willing

and true?

I love this man like

a needle to an

arm

it might be an

addiction

but this love

can't do me

any harm

Are you ready for

this

boomerang effect

because I'm coming on

and coming back

strong

I love this man

like I love

my word

coming back

at you

with more love

Fast. . .

Hard. . .Light. . .And long

Breathe (Where Is He?)

Is it wrong for me to love you

the way that I do

to put you second to the One

who

blessed me with you

night and day I breathe you in

like the smoke that

clouded my memory

and cause me not

to see the true

you

Cccc ahhh ccc ahhh

Ccc ahhh ccc ahhh

I'm only doing what you would

have me to do when you

breathe into me

the breath from your lungs

to make them expand

with the love that is given

there ever after

Ccc ahhh ccc ahhh

Ccc ahhh ccc ahhh

Ccc ahhh ccc ahhh

I hear it again sounding like the echo

whispered in my ear

making my imagination go

to the left, to the left

Ccc ahhh ccc ahhh

Ccc ahhh ccc ahhh

Ccc ahhh ccc ahhh

Ccc ahhh ccc ahhh

I can feel you now

all over my skin

as our skin melts with heat and you don't mind

me playing with you

laying with you

rubbing you and caressing you

that's all I wanna do

Well. . .maybe not all

but you know?

Ccc ah ccc ah

Ccc ahhh ccc ahhh

Ccc ahhh ccc ahhh

Are we there yet? I

don't. . .

think. . .

so. . .

one more time?

Ccc ahhh ccc ahhh

Ccc ahhh ccc ahhh

Ccc ahhh ccc ahhh

thank you

for giving me

a mental vision of

what is about to. . .happen

Ccc ahhh ccc ahhh

Ccc ahhh ccc ahhh

Wait. . .what the f***

I didn't get to cum

did you?

Bullisht Talk (Telephone Drop Late Night Call)

With my ankles wrapped around

Your shoulders in the midst of

Getting that high that we both want

The telephone does its little

Diddy of

I Got What You Need

Uh huh

"who da fuck could that be"

Ringing your phone at this

Late hour

I'm laying right here

So hell

I know it ain't me

"Hey baby what it be like?

My mind wonders "hey baby what it be like"

It be like " I want you"

"But I'm busy right now

Call me back

If your man let you

Around two"

"Don't hang up"
"Naw bitch I gots to go"
What you fail to realize
Is that I'm up in this
"piece with my other hoe"
"your other hoe?!
Yeah bitch that's what I said
Now if you will excuse me
A brothah tryn' to
Get some head"

"dirty bastard I thought I was the dime"
"You know you are baby
That's why I gave you some time"
But keep in mind that
A dime is just
Ten cents
This one right here
I got now
Is my
Hundred dollar queen
Now you know

Where all my money spent

Muthaf****

I ought to kick yo @$$

Come on over

That should be more fun

And will make the

Stroke last

Dirty bastard you said I was

The only one

Yeah that night you were

But I also told you

I had a loaded gun

You comin' or what?

You can if you wanna

I would call you out your name

But that would be

Disrespecting yo mamma

Dirty low down

Good for nothing
Snake in the grass
I still ought to
Come over just to
Kick yo @$$

I said you can if you wanna
But I ain't gonna
Stop what I'm doing
This hoe is too good
To get out of
So I'mma get through screwing

You can stay on the line
If you want
And hear what you
Missing from "dad...dy"
Or hang up cumin
All by your damn self
Thinking about you
Could have had me

Naw pawtnah that's the
Other way around
Remember I'm that
Hundred you missed
Out on
And there are other niggas
In town

But you see
You wouldn't
Know real from counterfeit
If it walked
Up and slapped
You in the face

So funk you
Punk muthaf****
I know where you live
I got your
Number
So I'm callin back
Same time

Same place

Dat's all right hoe

I'm still swimmin' in it

And you gave me nothing

But **bullisht talk**

Time for you to say bye bye hoe

I don't give a f***

WALK. . .

Buried Treasure (A Plea To Be Found)

My body aches for you

my clit craves your tongue

I let no other man's tongue

touch the jewel that belongs

to you

Underneath the ruby red

jewel lies a pearl

That an oyster couldn't

contain

The sweet concoction

Of an emerald

Saying "go, go, go"

deeper still

Like an octopus

with suction that holds

tight its prey

just to find that sapphire

shine so brightly in the

middle

of the ocean's bay

Ohhhhh how my seas

had a good time
riding the waves
that felt more like a
waterfall
with opal settings that
attached themselves to crystals
then my body still aches
for you
and my clit craves your tongue
I let no other man's tongue
touch the jewel
that belongs to you
so my chest
is waiting to be
unlocked by you
so that you can fully
enjoy
the jewels
in your **buried treasure**

Can I Rock Withchu?

Can I rock withchu day or night?

Night or day?

In the middle of a. . .

Ummm, reading class or stage play?

I wanna rock witchu

Five to 10 or

10 toes down

Let's have each other's back

From the clouds all the way down

To your Achilles heel

Back up to the top of your head

Knowing every follicle non

Numerical

Numerical

Can I rock withchu?

Rock withchu I can

In the daytime

Noon time

Midnight hour

From January

February

March

And all the April showers

I gotta beef that I need to get off my

Shoulders

It's not a burden

Because I don't wanna be

A burden

And saturate your id

With a misunderstanding of rocking witchu

When there is no one else I want to rock with.

Can I withchu, rock?

Witchu, can I roll?

Rock, can I witchu?

Can't Sleep

I'm not going to curse, I'm not going to shout, I'm just going to tell him what I heard so that he can decide if he wants out. It shouldn't have to be his decision, it should be mine ~ I'mma give him a few chances this time to stop lying. . .you see there came a call this morning about 15 minute to four ~ he and the female were talking about Facebook with him saying what he says to me "don't start" now to find a way to handle this situation without blowing my cool. . .in knowing that once again, I've been made to look like the fool *smdmfh* but even on Friday nights he's usually with me or talking on the phone with me laying across his bed; this has only been the second time that he didn't make it this way with his apologetic tone telling me he sorry. . .I'mma see what kind of lie he'll put into this story.

I've had enough of the games even enough of the "I love you's." I've shown him off to friends telling them this love was true. . .should have known better to believe a preacher's son, at best to me right now this clown, I guess it's time for me to go and lay my tired ass back down. . .LOL. . .**can't sleep.**

Challenge My Heart

Lavender body wash to relax my senses

With chamomile added to

Block out my defenses

No terry cloth to wrap this soft temple

Of mine

But plenty of shea butter not to make me sweat

Yet also shine

A dash of scent behind the ears

On the wrists

Behind the knees

And the crevice of the elbow

Oh! Let us not forget

Behind the neck

Where the lips may go. . .

No stockings tonight

Not even time for those silly grins

But before the night is through

You'll pull the lever shouting

"JACKPOT" to see who really wins

I'm in a purple mood and for me

That's the new color of love on my part
I'm not out to use you
I just want your time
To **challenge my heart**
I'm not going to say that I'm the right one
I'll let my actions speak for me
I've been craving you from the start
I just desire you to be
That challenge for my heart
I refuse to chase
Is the thought as I put on the red
That piece is layered with lace
And the idea of dark chocolate
Will be thrown on the bed
No polish on the nails
But lightly spread gloss on the
Object that speaks
Please challenge my heart because
I haven't heard from you in weeks
I breathe you every moment
I whisper your name

I close my eyes and hope
That you are doing the same
I wait patiently for your call just to
Hear your tone
On the other end
I want you to be the one to challenge my heart
So that I can be to you
More than just a friend.
Ooops! The new color of love is purple
And once again I had to start
So I put the red back
the one layered with lace
Giving you time to challenge my heart
Waiting for you to show up at my place
You took the red eye which dropped at seven
You had made wonderful plans
Which was on your part
Then I finally knew when you made it
You already challenged
And captured my heart

Cipher (A Kwansaba)

Close your eyes and follow the moon

Walk around the sun and fly free

The stars carry you to the sky

The earth's flowers are full of you

Cipher my heart to carry you daily

Out stretch my arms to hold you

Rest while the days come to night

Circle (My Dilemma)

Opening spaces for you just to

come in

into my empty space

to fill it up

and pour it out again

with me you could be

more than the man

you want to be

some of the man you ought

to be

all of the man

you need to be

for me

split down the middle

it becomes half

half of what was said

half of what was thought

which leaves no room

in that empty space

for another heart

erase. . .

erase. . .

erase. . .

starting over to make the

circle complete

completely. . .

correct, outstanding

simply. . .neat

120

120

120

is the full scale of your

inner being

glow

while I'm still empty

90

slow. . .

cut cross ways

it's the same as half

it's just split in a different

direction

so

here is my math

a ball is round like the earth

a circle is flat

when drawn on paper

what's a circle have to do with a ball?

a ball holds gravity while falling

a circle lies still when drawn

120

120

120

absolutely

nothing at all

that circle is still empty

and I'm going around in it

as you're put second to none

the circumference of my circle

120

120

120

360

One

Cream

He has me at night where I can't

sleep but

walking around with the lights on

looking for him

it must be crazy

this thing called

infatuated lust

or mesmerizing dream

got me singing like Prince

Sha~boogie~bop

Cream

I would love to get on top

of his mile high

extended play

of a rollercoaster

and then bump a beat

in his jeep

screaming out his name with the fire

in our eyes

and heat that we can feel ten

millimeters

down stream

as we pull over

he made my body **cream**

got me singing like Prince

Sha~boogie~bop

and when I say red light

he will stop

when I say yellow light

he will take it slow

and when I say green light

he will go

when I say switch lanes

he will give the signal

when I say pit stop

he will take a break

just to see and feel me cream

all over the place

I couldn't stop the flow of

his magnetic force

I wouldn't stop it if I really wanted to

where I am beautiful to

him being a handsome boo

riddle me that

or riddle me a dream

got me singing like Prince

Sha~boogie~bop

Cream

we are not talking 31 flavors here

we are talking only

one that is sweet

morning, noon or nighttime

he can have it any time

I will be his treat

a voice that electrifies

and arms that are hard as a rock

he'll have me singing like

Prince

all night long

Sha~boogie~bop

Cream

Emperor's Ways

Let it be known that once

I laid my eyes on you

you were to be mine as the very essence

of

the spirit that you possess

I took your breath away

You stood still

your heart beat out of control

as you did your best to maintain

the fire that burned

on the inside

and yet, I was not enough

ice

to cool the feverish

temp

that boiled

to your deepest core

I

too

felt the steam that

water could not contain

for I am only

a mere image of your

imagination

captured by the fleet

of a welding soul

that would not let go

until said so. . .

I

too

am one desiring to be kept

wrapped in the magnificent glow

of your after

with the sigh of relief

that sound like wind chimes in the

breeze

caution trees without leaves

fall golden to earth's

surface

I

am one

with the **emperor**

give me a moment to

meditate

on your inner sanctuary

where

I

am the most

comfortable

being. . .

as in human

not humane but

being gently insane

causing a ripple through my body

like a river flow

let it be known

that once I laid my eyes on you

I'm only doing

what needs to be done. . .

tasting with my mind

Face Me (Quiet Storm Trilogy For "You")

With my face toward the

Ceiling I hear

The drops

On my window

As I await your

Existence

To **face me**

Cleverly with the

Boldness of

A demi-god

Oh! Lord what have

I gotten

Myself into?

All I wanted was

For him to face

Me

My quiet storm

You. . .

With my face turned to the wall

With thoughts

Of lighted gas

That brightened

The night

With his hands cupping

Those mountains

That belong to him

Uh huh

You know the ones

In that circular motion

With his fingers

I still can't

Stand the rain

Against my window

So I close my eyes to reminisce

Of once was

His rounded

Thigh

Draped around the ever

So tender and soft skin

Oh Lord

What have I gotten myself into

Again?

With my face

Downward facing the pillow

That quiet storm has now

Enraged my spirit

To let my

Demi-god in

With a definite arch in my back

And a

Curl to his toes

That quiet storm got a little

Bit louder

Sounds of

Thunder roars

Oh Lord

What have I gotten myself

Into

His quiet storm

Face me

You. . .

Back to the ceiling

I turn to

See the sweat roll

From his chin

Oh Lord

I ask

Continuously

What have I gotten myself

Into again?

He travels down that main street

And enter my courts

A time or two

Ahhhhhhhh

That feels good

I'm only hoping

This could happen

With my

Demi god

To my quiet storm

Facing me...

Facing...YOU

Four Chambers

When my heart won't let go

it allows me to speak my peace

then remains silent until the other

heart is connected

to feel the same vibration

as the heartbeat on the **first chamber**.

When my heart won't let go

it allows me to breathe

every word into my lungs

back into your mouth when I exhale

with a kiss~ the kind of kiss the **second**

chamber of your heart can feel.

When my heart won't let go

it allows me to see the man behind

the mask who wants love just as much

as your **third chamber** can hold

then overflow

with the exceptional

flutter that makes your mind wonder

I'm doing my best to slow down

so that you can have time for your

hearts to catch up to mine.

Chamber four is bursting

with so much admiration

that it covers the other

three overpowering the mind

to just give into the love

that is only for you.

And when my heart won't go

will your heart allow me inside

long enough to heal what's broken

to love again and become yours?

FREQUENCY

My ears are ringing loudly

with my eyes closed ~ my breath

slow and steady

my mind is empty

filled with those

that have no business occupying

my space

so I empty it with the sound

of

waves entering a universe

far beyond the eye can see

I can hear the sound of you

whispering

in a low vibration

that

breaks the barrier

of my soul

like crystals.

Rubies of the

Muladhara 40 hertz

whereas the canary yellow

Alpha stands 10 Hertz bursts

Anahata emerald loves the heart it beats for

my vibrations beats for

my soul mating in the distance.

what sound can be heard

when you close your eyes

to keep your ears from ringing?

I need you in my **frequency**

FROM GRAVE TO GRAVESITE

I poured black coffee in my tea

sugar in my flour canister

so blindly

tea in my water bottle

and the water

in the milk carton

milk in the juice jar

and juice on my chocolate bar

I'm extremely . . .wasted

used up like a number

2 pencil with the lead

as dull as

a double edge. . .

I told the story of

Heaven and Hell

that no man can put me in or under

because they are not perfect either

I never said that I was. . .

In time there will be no more

black coffee in my tea

sugar in my flour canister

tea in my water bottle

water in my milk carton

milk in the juice jar

and juice on my candy bar

you won't be able to tell me

I'm extremely. . .wasted

lipstick on my eyes

eyeliner on my lips

rouge on my fingernails

and polish on my cheeks

used up like a quill

pen that was

sharp

as a razor blade

I told the story of

Heaven and Hell

you still have neither to

put me in

because you still are not perfect either

I never said I was. . .

after time there will be no more

lipstick on my eyes

eyeliner on my lips

rouge on my fingernails

and polish on my cheeks

where the illusion of

love will

send me to an early grave

and my gravestone will read

"here lies a woman who died

of a broken heart"

from grave to gravesite when you see it

keep walking. . .

G.A.M.E. (Giving All My Energy)

I brought my "A" game

To the table

And there was no turning back

Back from the

Righteous bull

That was thrown at

me during the course

Of the

Three round bout

In the ring

Giving the first punch

TKO

And back up again

I brought my second

"A" game to the bases

As they were loaded

Ready and waiting

To be unloaded

As I waited for a

Response

To. . .

"hey baby, bring it on"

Okay,

Where you want me slugger?

The third "A" game

I made a pit stop

To refuel

So that I could

Give

All

My

Energy

To his

Energies

Just so that he could

keep up

HERE WE GOOOOOO!

My "A" game is good

While I raced

Around the track

Bareback~

Oooooops did I do that?

My "A" game is wild

As I skate to his

Rhythms

That has him

Whimpering like

A child

My "A" game is golden

As I wore him

Around

My neck

Like a brace

Giving

All

My

Energy

To mesh with his

Energies

Where

A simple line

Mark leaves a trace

Of

Ooooh's and ahhhh's

Escaping from

The succulent

Small curve of the lips

While the ocean's

Waves moves

The motion of

The sink ships in hips

My "A" game is bad

Meaning

Greatness

In every sense of the word

Giving

All

My

Energy

To melt his

Energies

I'm the

Boss b****

That's what I heard

Giving

All

My

Energy

Just to match

His energies

And we glowing

Just the same

Giving

All

My

Energy

Just to drain

And restore

His energies

I just brought

And doubled my

"A" game

GET PASSED THIS

Pardon me while I not say

a word and I have the right

to remain silent at all cost

Pardon me while I reach

way

into my future in

order to understand my past

pass the hurt

pass the quilt

pass the sin

pass the love and pain

just don't pass me by

when it's my

turn to receive love

I miss the past love

I miss the past caress

I miss the past hugs and kisses

I miss the past

I miss you. . .

I passed up what I missed

pass the midnight hour

pass the morning dawn
pass the moon's rising
pass the setting of the sun
pardon me while I shed a tear
of being filled with emptiness
Say huh?!

Pass the empty cup to be filled
pass the pain
pass the scars
pass the fear
pass the love devoured heart
pass the preconception of
It is what it is: the past
Leave it where it can no longer be found
It's time to heal

HAVE YOU GIVEN THANKS TODAY?

Giving thanks is a thing learned
Learning is something that is given
Given the opportunity to be concerned
Concerned about the life you're living.

Living while the day is dawning
Dawning to see the sun rise
Rise to see the sun shining
Shining to know the glow in eyes.

Eyes that says "I love you"
You to say it in return
Return the love only you can do
Do it to know what you can earn.

Earn a thought or feeling thereof
Of a price you didn't have to pay
Pay attention to those you love
And ask yourself
Have you given thanks today?

Today is a day of thanksgiving

Giving is an action that's granted

Granted is a prize as you are living

And living his breath you have chanted

Chanted is sayings that you mouth with your tongues

Tongues are used to speak words

Words are definitions of different songs

Songs are heard through God's hummingbirds.

Hummingbirds are winged animals of the air

Air is unseen wind that you feel

feel is a slight touch that belongs there

There is where the heart is real.

Real is when something happens for you to think "Okay"

Okay is fine and you're all right

Right is asking, have you given thanks today?

And today will become a peaceful night.

Stacey Barlow

HE MADE ME CRY

Not the average kind to bring a

tear to my eye

not the painful kind of hurt

but joyful news

he made me cry

with a silent demeanor as he

asks

"Are you okay?'

I choked back the tears

to reply "Yes"

in dismay

the burning sensation that was

felt thousands of miles

away from soul to soul

I'm in love ya'll

my secret is about to unfold

finding ways to get to my king in time

after all that has been said and

done

the sweet caress of spirit to spirit

constantly to him

I run

it's too good to be true

astoundingly a dream

I don't want to awake from

back to forth, forth to back

side to side

inside and out

here I come

it was hard to hold back

the joy I was feeling

as he was diving deeper

into me

I couldn't breathe for a second when he said

"with you I'm falling in love

madly"

I was putty in his hands for the

rest of the night

and I don't know why

but those words

will burn forever in

my soul

and that's how ~ he made me cry

HEAD PIECE (Fantasy Of Mr. Big)

I lay a top of the quilted

pallet

awaiting for my prince to arrive

and yet he

says his good morning

hellos as well as

his good night goodbyes

enamored by the way

he moves delighted

by the

sensual stands

of his piece

awkward hands

gave way to

head

My turn to rule his world and make

him fall

prey to ice cream

dreams and melt

into another

dimension of sighs

cries and

oh whys?

of my head burn not rope

just a piece

to tie him over

until the next

go round

I'm so ready to give

him a piece

of Heaven

that he has taken

for granted only

for a time

that won't be forgotten

in the back of his

mind

he's wanting more

but bites his lip

and holds his

peace

for reasons unsure

glad he loves the way

I give

last time and once

more

I want to be in his stead

laying flat on his back

screaming out my name

with all his heart and soul

wanting more. . .

head

I NEED A PEN TO MY PAD

I held that **pen** for the longest time

wondering if I could find the necessary

words to scribe and put down on the

empty piece

I shook the pen but no

ink came out

I pulled it apart to look inside

still no ink came out

put it back together and a little

ink spilled onto my fingers

but still it wasn't enough

to

pen*e*trate

the pad that I wanted to

write on so desperately

opened the pen back up

to blow inside to get

what particles of dried ink

I thought may be left inside

still empty

so I discarded that pen

Stacey Barlow

to begin again

to write

found another

to ink my pad ~ feather light

slim, yet easy to hold

but tickled between my

thumb and middle finger

that's not the way to hold a pen but for the time

being it felt so right

I dropped it once

I dropped it twice

Damn...maybe I

need...

feather light

had to be dipped

but I got tired of dipping

so I licked the tip one last

time

to dry the ink with my

tongue and for some reason

the ink on that pen

begged for me

to keep writing
but there was nothing yet on
the pad
still empty
the next pen had a
Silver band around
the center
written on the side
truly and forever yours
I smiled at the thought
of this pen
giving me the satisfaction
the will keep me
writing for days
and nights
sweat running down my brow
as I bring pen to mind
my mind released
energies that my
fingers didn't know
but that pen did
and as I wrote

Stacey Barlow

I came and came so more

my mind released

what my pad

could not comprehend

I came and came some more

my pen guided me to my fantasies

untold

and opened up a new

world

that my

id lost

control

no time for conversation

no time for idle threats

no time for revelations

no time for watered down secrets

I need a pen to my pad

that will not lie to me

I need a pen to my pad

that will show me truths

I need a pen to my pad

that will show me the future

No more emptiness

of unbridled youth

the pen kept flowing

as tears flowed

down my cheeks of

a love that I've known

for so long

that love never left me

from heart to fingers

to bone

this pen that I picked up

is the best I ever had

to continue to

scribe my

past, present, and future

and I still think

I need a pen to my pad

I WANT YOUR. . .

I be he

he be me

me and he be we

around complications of your love

and all **I want is your**

time. . .

Time to reminisce on

days that are well spent

Not "spent" as in

I cum once, cum twice

cum hence

under you

as I be he

he be me

me and he be we

around complications of your soul

all **I want is your**

love. . .

love that takes me beyond

another space

but to another level

which only you can

follow

I cum once, I cum twice

I swallow

the essence of a

dream that you have

just given me

above you

as I be he

he be me

me and he be we

around complications in your eyes

all **I want is your**

mind. . .

to think about how

much of me

you can have

eternally. . .

everlasting. . .

completely. . .

I am all for you

while another

tries to come in and
steal what doesn't
belong to him
I cum once, I cum twice
as my vision goes
dim
because I desire to become
one with you
and not him
here is the complication
all **I want is your**
heart. . .
to beat for me and me
alone ease my troubled
mind
to let me know
I am your own
I be he
he be me
me and he be we
all **I want is your**
hand. . .

to hold when you are scared

and there are no more

complications

to see

I be he

he be me

me and he be we

you and I become one

Marry me. . .

IF I WERE HIS (Daydreaming)

If I were his

And he were mine

There would be plenty

Of

Precious jewels sprinkled across the

Chambers of his heart

To fill him with nothing

But me

If I were his

And he were mine

Glitter would be the name

Of his shampoo

To wash away the negativities of the day

So that my fingers can

Caress the scalp of the

Everlasting mind of the man

I call. . .nature

If I were his

And he were mine

I'd shower him with

Kisses in the moonlight

And morning til dawn
So that my lips would linger
On the nape of his neck
Until he comes home
If I were his
And he were mine
The very essence of his soul
Would cry my name
And be forever in his spirit
If he were to make me his
He would know it
He would know It for all eternity
If I were his
I would be his queen

IN THE MEANTIME

In the meantime

I am his meantime

and in his past time

he passes the time

with me being his meantime

In his meantime

he lives to see what he

can devour and use

for his future time while

searching for his

past time in the

meantime

I will be

walking out of the door

smelling exceptionally well

a fragrance that has never been

aired before makes me wonder

what the occasion is

of today in the meantime

while I passed the time hoping

that it will be the same

when he walks back through that door

but in the meantime

and in between time

I digress forever other

situations that was put upon me

to deal with for that meantime

I can't stand being his meantime

it's as if he's searching for

something better

than what he has

right. . .now

I'm not saying that I'm the best

But I. . .am. . .the. . .best

But in the meantime

I digress

to look head on from the past

to become his future

when he says he's

not looking for anything

but another meantime experience

with me

In the meantime

I am his meantime

and in his past time

he passes the time

thinking of someone else

who is not me

So in my meantime

he's my past time

I'll pass the time

utilizing my meantime

and my meantime

is taken up by

whatever it means to pass the time

INDESCRIBABLY AMAZING

Let me kiss thy lips upon stories untold

where travels of the mind

upon the eye of beauty

is sold

Let me touch the face where

cherry blossoms lay

in the midst of all there is

my king to play

My knight and shining

armor come rescue me

from the pits of

degradation

even from Hell's Kitchen

to the cooling of

fresh spring air

born of a new creation

create in me ~ amazingly

a human of habit abound by love

indescribably decadent

from stars, moon, a flight

to the skies above

misbehaved

punishable

at best

going full circle

five, nine, 12

no time to rest

amazing how the body craves for you

at midnight unsung

back to that full circle

without stopping until

The break of dawn

I want to make sweet love to you until

your spirit is connected to mine

as two becomes one

and spirits are joined

indescribably amazing

where there is

no space between time

no time between space

we forget where we are

or where we have been

Only to open up more

freely and

allow the extra flow of

love to come in

I be you

you be me

us be we

my king. . .

indescribably amazing

INFINITY

In the morning when I wake to see your face

To feel the best of you that love can place

Even life of hurt can burn

Heart of gold will surely turn

My love alive is yours

Four corners of the mind

Set me free

I desire to be your kind

Infinity

INVISIBLE

The words can you see me now

are

still in the back of my mind

and the mind is

never seen but

always heard because

words are always spoken

take away the inevitable

where feelings are

obscured

hear me now, see me now

feel me now

say

I won't remain

invisible

KUTABARE (Devil's F*ckery)

I opened that door to let you in and you

led me to that playground

where

I couldn't get off and there

you continued to play me

over so I found a way to

Go there and

Be strong

Kutabare

Emotions ran high

where friends are pitted against each other

and you know what you are doing

but minds are not as weak as

you perceive them to be

Kutabare

when kutabare steps in

no man's mind is safe

from speculation to

what can happen next

I'm that chick your

momma warned you about

you...don't...know...me
so watch out
you think you might
have worn me down
and tried to destroy me
but when I don't respond
to your advances
you can't get mad
go to the next one you
think
who's not paying attention
Oh! Did I forget to mention
kutabare ketsunoana
yes, I'm just that angry
so I'll say it again
in a different tongue
and it will be heard
and you can go
zakennayo

LAST FIRST KISS

The tenderness of such sweet

lines

that won't lead to sorrow

the softness of two

parted ways

that will linger until

tomorrow

In between thoughts

of undisguised bliss

my king whispers in my ear

about his dream of his

last

first

kiss

with such passion inside

that will make my spirit burn

wanting my

first

kiss to

last

from the after taste

will make me yearn

for a much deeper

connection

from eyes to hands

to the back of my neck

Oh Lord have mercy on my soul

he has put me in seclusion

an emotional wreck

I could feel is breath trickling down

my spine

and back up from hand to fist

as he continued

to whisper

his erotic dream of his

last

first

kiss

with me

a new beginning

has emerged from

him

purged with

body to slightly

damped skin

feeling the heat

of the

last

first

kiss

is where the magic

begins

not stopping

until he gets his fill

of his

last

first

kiss

explaining still to me

power

over

will

deep in my passion

a sound escaping

from the

abyss

as he goes

further within

for his

last

first

kiss

LET'S PLAY (Me, Her and Him)

Tapping my foot as I walked up the

stair well to your place

in my mind the thought passed

I'm going to love you so good

I'm going to make you forget

every woman

you've ever been with

in your space

we start with a simple dinner

and top it off with

strawberries and cream

then walked in

another surprise

you were giving me

the girl of my dreams

you promised the night would

be special and there was nothing

to be afraid of

back to back, front to

front

top to bottom

all different types of love
I want to go first
because he loves the way I ride
while you do your thing as you
watch on the side
I look at you and beckon
for you to come to me
with him in the middle
and then you slide underneath
the three of us
on a high to climax
we all trying to reach
him in back of you
with me on the bottom
you also desire to be pleased
while we both got him
our poetic rhythms heighten
our speed
where we all get wild and it
explodes to greed
I'm going to love you so good
That you'll

forget the other women you have been with

time for girl ~ girl action

to a handful of others

it's not a myth

in the forefront of my mind

I wanted to have her

and he wanted me to have her too

as he sat in the corner with a video camera

saying, "baby, make it do what it do"

he knew I was good at

some tongue action

so he wanted her to know

that I could come

with that satisfaction

double the pleasure

while tripling to the floor

didn't need any more surprises

then came a knock at the door

with a grin on her face

and a grin on his as he

dropped the bomb. . .

Damn! Where did he come from?

LITTLE LAURA (Wood)

Walking the streets paved with gold

on the way from school **Little Laura**

would pick up broken glass from a bottle

stepping over a pipe in the crack of the sidewalk

Little Miss Wood

skipped home passed 34th street

around the alleyway

to avoid the stench of

unburied bodies lying in the gutter

wondering could or would

one be that forgotten uncle

wouldn't she like to know

the clock strikes five ~ time's up

She rushes home to greet her

other siblings waiting for her to tell

the story of the misguided soul that she ran into

four days before

gotta get supper going

study

and ready for bed

she's only 10

3 a.m. Little Laura would
rise and stir to prepare
the others for school
or wherever they planned to be
Little Laura would
fix breakfast, lunch, dinner
one by one would she allow herself to
give into the daydream she long to dream
of easier days
little did Laura know
her days were easy

She would, Miss Wood, if she could
take them to the streets that were paved
with gold
but there was no time
she was only
10
A painted mural of her face
on a wall as she walked by
she smiled at the thought
that she would, Miss Wood, if she could

make it easier to recognized misguided faults

that were not her own

Little Laura Wood

would, if she could

She was only 10

but never made it back home

Stacey Barlow

MAY I TRY AGAIN TONIGHT?

As I ease next to you

While I place my hand upon your

. . .

The sound you make

Takes me on a natural high

I enter that

Outer link

Of the forbidden zone

As I guide my finger

Tips

To your

. . .

The whimper escapes your lips

As you part them

Slightly quick

I mount

So coyly

Like a tiger on your

Powerful

Speed. . .

Granted I'm not ready for you

Yet

Because I want

To play

A little while

There

I love it

When your eyes roll back in your head

As I

Run my fingers through your

. . .

The motion of your body

Is like

Beats to a

Song

I wish so much that you would

Part your lips again

So I can taste your

. . .

I'm still not

Ready to explore

You yet

Please put your

Fingers there

To get me

...

I inhale

And exhale

All in the same token

Right?

So I'll ask you once

May I try again

Tonight?

Honestly, your skin

Tastes like

Honey suckle

I could go all night

If my knees didn't

...

I want you

Inside of me like nobody's

Business

So lock the door

Turn off the phone

And let's get

With this

You know you

Want me

Like I want you

Simple and

Plain,

Right?

So I'll ask for the

Last time

May I try again

Tonight?

MIRROR

Can you see me? A revealing reflection

of surface from

the inside out

I am so you

as you look back at me to touch the same

hand

that feels like

that hand belongs there

with the eyes of the soul

that tells the whole story

in full spectrum

filling the cypher

up like calm water

under certain lighting

reflecting that ray

within

you are so me

building that frame that

once was

surrounded by the foundation

of truth

you look inside me

I look inside you

we see each other

the foundation ends

with us

staring back at

each other

We...blend

like twins

having the same breath thinking

the same thought

finishing

the same

sentences

I am so you

you are so me

looking at each other through

space and time

two spirits collide

with ease

watching as time and space

gives us a chance to

fight for

what's rightfully ours. . .

love. . .

~you and me against the world

MY CASUALTY

EXCELLENT MEMORY:

I knew how to spell at three

knew how to read in pre school

but I went to a school for

"gifted" children

whose brain activity

was above the norm

where the grownups would

teach, uplift, inspire

and protect us

from harm

That's a lie

I remember my first

kiss at

16

Yes there are still some

of those left

but the innocence

was taken away

at the mere age of five

where my body

and mind was put to

death

The truth is a survivor

SELECTIVE MEMORY:

Half my brain tells me

not to go on

but the other half tells me

that I need to be strong

strong for what?

the right love

love is so overrated

and I died years ago

trying desperately to forget

exes

numbers one through four

but they always seem to come back

and haunt

me

every detail of what

was done for them

but what was done to me

what did I do wrong

but love unconditionally

My body is tired; my brain needs rest

I had six stand in line

in my mind

because of

their wrong doings

and I treated them well

feeling that they were all

angels at first

but they were only

men from hell

I've been through the fire

Seven made me choke to death

I felt him inside me

burning

my spirit, mind, and body

tried to come alive again

I needed to release

and let go

for the last time

feeling a bit

lightheaded

my casualty

has no body

count

that's so divine

you'll never know what I'm thinking

AMNESIA:

I forgot the names

of the

Exes

maybe this one will

stay in my memory

not my

casualty. . .

Hello, and what is your name?

MY EVERYTHING (You Are)

With life you breathe in air

exhaling negativity that behooves

you to the

fullest

the mind takes you away

to place you never want to

return from

~paradise

Bringing sunshine into your heart

that can't be replaced

everything is everything

and **everything is you**

as days go by you continue

to

walk the walk of many men

but you do it so

differently

in space and time

beyond the stars

that take you away from the things

that your mind can't ponder

but it sends you right back to

~paradise

as it still is

everything is everything

and everything is you

your everything is love

hold on to the promise

of

what you can bring to

your life

and life will bring

it back to you

~paradise

and **you are**

Everything

MY EVERYTHING (The Rejection)

The love making is

greatness

for me

but he doesn't think

so

I love this man

to pieces

and he doesn't believe it

go figure

yet he whispers the words

"you're my woman, I'm your nigga"

understand this

I know exactly what that means

no one else can get it

and you can't tie me down

type of thing

He takes me on a

ride that won't ever stop

from my head to my toes

back to the middle and

over the top

I love the way he gives

me that look when

he's ready

for play

but to him I'm too

much or

so he says

any time of the day

I desire to be

all that I can for him

and he for me

as he makes my soul sing

he makes my spirit fly for

he is my

everything

He holds me in a way

that makes my body

quiver in his arms

my mind is free to explore

the power of his charms

He made me capture stars

that doesn't show

in the day light

and reach for goals

beyond belief

and love that

hides

out of mind

out of sight

Reach for me my king

I'm here for you

when you want me

as your lover

your ride and die chick

your woman

while I want

to

also make your soul

sing

to make your body

and spirit

reach a leveled

high

to make you moan

my, my, my, my

my, my, my

I want to be a part of you

as you are

a part of me

my king

just trying to let you know that

you are my everything

one day I will

be a part of you

as you are a part of me

And NO ONE

will come in between

what is yours

my king

at this moment in

time

plus forever

I desire to

be

your everything

MY LOVER

You keep me up at night

wrapped in essence of the invisible

--you

I can't imagine not having

--your essence inside of me

which is to ache for

the thought of being

coasted on an island

breeze with the waves

clashing against the sounds of

our minds

--you

lover of my imagination

has awaken the senses

only you can unlock

the very core of my being

that whispers. . .I

belong to

--you

I cry out to

--you I beg of

--you to

make me yours

until I can't

--take

no more

of your silent

screams only I can hear

that makes me cater to

--you

Now. . .that. . .I have

decided to be. . .bonded

--by

what is meant to be

I patiently wait

for

--you to make me yours

in the dark of night

I fall prey to

visions of

love

everlasting. . .

give me that moment

to show

--you

I can be true

and in the end

I patiently wait

for

--you

to call me

yours

MY MOJITO

It went from the bottom of my toes

to the tip of my head when I swallowed every word

you said

I tilted back just to catch my breath so that

the blood would rush in another direction

and man!

Did it take its time about doing so

It almost left a bitter taste in my mouth

until I

licked my lips and the sweetness of your voice

made my tongue more wet.

I swallowed again only harder this time

and tasted your salt at the bottom of the glass

your salt burned my soul like fire making me

want to lie down

and feel what you feel and desire more.

I drank you enough to make me drunk

and take a stroll down thumb street

while thinking of you.

I'll have to know if I was a fool for drinking you

and letting you enter me without permission

but still making me feel good like

I

needed it

Mojito I'm giving you my time

since you were kind enough to ask for it

I'll drink you every day if I have to

And each time I open you

Your wisp welcomes me

to another dimension.

I'm ready to drink the rest of you.

Y cada vez que te tengo

Submerged en deseos

Tu suspiro me invita a

Otras dimensiones es shi do

Queiendo tomar cada gota

De tu mas preciado liquido

El que desprende tu cuerpo como la

NEW SHERIFF IN TOWN

Tall ~ yet stern when it is about time

To

Take care of business

The right way

This man can possibly catch bullets

With his teeth

On any given day

Fighting crime ~ taking care of his

Falling in line outside the rest

He is one in a million

But at his best ~ he IS love

UNCONTEST(ED)

Unconditional boundaries he can surely

Cross

Because

I have given him permission

To

Put away other

LOSS(ES)

There is a **new sheriff in town**

And

Oooooweeeee!

I can't wait to file a charge

Against the one who broke my heart

Just so I can see this sheriff

In action

Do his part in

Mending this broken

Heart of miiiine

exhale

This new sheriff in town

You'll have to see for yourself

And you'll say the same

Everyone in agreement?!

He entered into my life

He saw. . .he conquered. . .he came

NO MORE FOOTPRINTS (2:15 a.m.)

I let the memories of old shade my heart

where he wasn't able to come in

and sup with me and

me with him because

I didn't want him to walk all over my heart

and leave **footprints**

he wondered the same

the first set of prints

I took baby steps to insure that it was

love but, it was that so called puppy love

that all had us excited from time to time

the second set of prints

was the one of "if you love me

you would" can't stand

the pressure

the third set of prints was

"If you don't know what you're talking about

don't say a word ~ keep your

mouth shut and

deeper in my heart the footprints

were dug

my fourth set by then I was just tired
and really didn't feel like walking so
the journey didn't last long
14 years later
a fifth pair decided to show
for the remainder of that time
was time well spent and long-lasting walk
of four until those
prints became tired, faded
and left in the sand where the wind
carried the footprints to Heaven **the sixth**
pair of prints were deeper still as during
the third set
was disappearing and the first set
continued to scar up
my heart
the sixth pair began to lag behind
whew!!! **The seventh pair**
ended up to be the meantime prints that
was known not for a long walk home two
years and seven months of agonizing pain
of the prints that

was the deepest if the six

eight sets of footprints

and I'm still not tired yet

these footprints

just need to know that I was there and not

leave an everlasting mark on

parts that stains the most

if there weren't any footprints

how will you know that I've been there?

no more drama

no more pain

all about the love

stepping lightly to not leave

a deep impression

but know I was there

no more footprints

I love you more

OPEN TO GIVE

Not too much ~ Not too little

but only just enough

to make you feel what

I feel ~ crushed

that's a spirit of unwillingness

to turn back to where I started

Not too much ~ Not too little

but only just enough

to make you see what I see

in your eyes

that sparkle when you smile

Not too much ~ Not too little

but only just enough

to make you hurt like

I hurt ~ I know it's

wrong to do so because

vengeance isn't mine

then deep inside I know I have

to give it to the ONE who can

and will protect me from the

dangers of my own mind

Not too much ~ Not too little

but only just enough

to make you shed a tear

Will I feel sorry for you?

The answer: I can't. . .

because you wouldn't do it

for me

So you see. . .I was **open to give**

but you were not ready to

receive

Stacey Barlow

QUALITY FABRIC OF A MAN

The word "beautiful" escapes from the

lips of his mouth each time

that moment is spent with you

in spite of all that surrounds the essence

of the world

the holding of the hand

the look in the eyes

through him as a mirror is at a

glance for you to see (MG)

The pulling out of chairs and

the opening of doors

while spending every waking moment

wondering if you are thinking of him

the embrace that's never ending with

a kiss that remains

for days for you and him (JM)

Traveling to and fro just to get a

glimpse of the woman that stands before

him

who adores the very

scent of the masculinity

he brings forth
with a closer embrace
that causes you not
to want to breathe
but you know you need to exhale
so that you as a woman
can pull him closer
into you (DW)

The nights under the stars
feeling the breeze
without a word
uttered to each other
but knowing that
you two belonged
a laugh that echoes
beyond the skies
that reach far above the Heavens
that makes even God smile
and you smile a
certain way (OJ)
A love beyond compare

where nothing can separate

the fun times

as he made love so easy and simple

dinner. . .movie. . .late night calls

love in a special way

that was cool to understand

and no games were played

even though left on good

terms

there was no feeling of hate (DH)

Constant calls and visits

just to be around you

support by the way of

one spoken word

plus the "I love you's"

a smile, a twinkle

a goodbye hug

and a voice like

a river stream

the height that

covers like a blanket

that when opened you are

set free (SE)

Last time when you're on borrowed time

the love that's hidden

behind the curtains

that are formed as eyelids

tears shed because

of hurt and pain

we have all been there

and he cared enough to

show his sensitive side

unlike the others

crying alligator tears

pretending to care when he really doesn't

but showing off outside

the skin

and love for you is there

nonetheless

so you give your all

on top of your very best

until you feel he has

found his way

you can love him until

his dying day

he will love you

in his grave

but you will never know it

because there won't be

anything left (DF)

My Goals Just Made Differences While Others Just

Delightfully Halted

Sacrifices Even Destitute Fame

RAIN DANCE

Raindrops on my pillow

As I dream of sunshine and the sun hides its smile

And open the clouds for a

Clear substance that's shaped

Like a tear falling from the Heavens above

And while it falls

Other follows in

A synchronized

Manner

Tickling the air

As it moves left to right

Sideways and even

Backwards

Playing the tips

To make their own

Music before

Water falls from the

Aqueous vapor in the

Atmosphere to the

Earth

Which makes its own beat like tiny conga drums

The drops play to their own rhythms
Continuing to dance into the asphalt
Until the sun comes out but
Until then. . .
It rained tonight
They will play and dance to their own rhythms
Continuing to dance into the asphalt
And the tear is no longer a tear but
A tiny puddle
Tonight. . .I heard the **rain dance**

RISE ABOVE (Hurricane Mix for "HIM")

The look in his eyes told me that

I belong to him and no one

else

for the night

there was none

like him

to quench my thirst

none like him to

leave my sight

He walks in with

that sway to his back side

Giving me that

look of "it's on tonight"

Be ready for it all

and get ready for a bumpy ride

We took our time

ever so slowly

to the point of

dripping

in sweat

Stacey Barlow

he gave me something to

think about

from the day our eyes met

Bold, suave,

absolutely divine

he became like a

world map

where I had to study every

curve

every line

Egypt the land of history

and gold

the traces of the eyes

where the secrets are told

Nigeria that sweet peace

of dark chocolate arose

there are more

secrets

in that place

that no one knows

Malaysia the beautiful

country as

a wide open space

to view

having a curved mountain

that would long be a part of you

Hawaii

is the island with

delightful beached sands

that caused for explosion

in those strongly

built hands

Thailand

brightened city

with tantalizing

colors of light

rise above

all the madness

And turn my quiet storm

into a **hurricane**

tonight

Fuji

a picture perfect

place

that you so

eagerly decided

to fix

as the rain came down

hard

and hail on the window

while you listened

intensely

as I thanked you for

giving me

your hurricane mix

SECRETS
(Before You Go ~ Collaboration w/ShadowStep Peace)

SHADOWSTEP PEACE

So streams

That "cream"

Melting sonnets like ice "screams"

Perky dreams

Coated in caramel

Shatter windows till sun-rays beam

Apple blossoms gleam

Was it what it seemed?

Discomfort noted

Befitting these jeans

Peel away

To the unseen

Definitely "My Lover" unlike Billy Jean

Sprinkle these kisses as chocolate vibes

Incite psychoactive

Aphrodisiac highs

Fade to a blend

Between your thighs

Drink in your desire

Speak to me in sighs. . .

Caress your reprise

Chiudi gli occhi il fare l'amore comincia

Close your eyes

Love making begins

Again reprise

Yet deeper still into your vibe

As pelvic thrusts

With force of course

Intensifies

Our **secret**. . .

****

STACEY BARLOW

standing behind me

with your hands

gently placed on

my curves

getting ready to

entice me with

your

Precious jewel

being careful not to

wake the neighbors

Ooooh! how I've

longed for your

lips to

touch the nape of my

neck

that makes my spine

quiver

whether you realize it or not

your dancing shadow

makes my

"in" come "out"

like a sweet honey

river

Stacey Barlow

Speak to me in the language

Of love

I like the way

you say what you say

let me revise

your reprise

say it again

Chiudi gli occhi il fare l'amore comincia

I spoke to you in sighs

as I

move to your rhythm

as you covered my

eyes

only to feel

the thrust of your

beginning

to my ever ending

demise

you defy me

In every sense of the word

Definitely Eros Forever Yours

all in my id

and out again

let us repeat this reprise

of secrets

that lies

between "us"

and "we"

can yet still

go deeper into this vibe

of melodic

creams and thrusts

go head

Intensify me

Our secret

SHADOW DANCING (Step Into My Dream)

It's the break of dawn

and I don't want the sun to shine

because I want to see what

your form is

against

my walls

I long to touch you

and hold you

but I only can trace the

silhouette

Of the shapeliness

of the profile

of your face

I can't wait until

nightfall

just to dance with you

and

really there is nothing

there

even when I call

your name
the lights go out
and you'll appear
up against
my walls again
There is no breath
there is no whisper
only a flame
from the flickering light
just to see the trace
of your silhouette
dancing with me
against my walls
I can't wait until
night falls
to see the trace of
you and your
silhouette
your face against
my face
just **dancing**
once you **step into my dream**

there is no turning back

from the **shadow** chasing

that I did against

my walls

waiting for you

to come along

during my night fall

Shadow you gave me a

dance

that I will never

forget

until

the break of

dawn

awaiting your

presence with the

flickering of

candle lights

and your silhouette

against my walls

tomorrow . . .

SHADOW RUN

I turn off the light

the next

night

to see my **shadow run**

instead the shadow

slid in between

what came

between

me and the

pen he was wanting

to

write with

hours on in

the middle of

my shadow run

ink spilled

warm all over

from tip

to ball point

shadow moved

down to run

score

some more

shadow can't make another

run

like I want to

because the moon is changing

on its axis

so the shadow

does a trot to trot

until the jar of ink

spills over

from climaxin'

shadow, I want to spoil

you

and not tease

shadow I want to keep

while your silhouette

is pleased

Shadow don't back

down

step up

And

make me feel your

breeze

shadow, shadow, shadow, oh shadow

I like the way you move

me

to the point of cold ice

subzero below

to freeze

the only way to

warm me

is to ink me dry

and let me hold your pen

until you make me

cry

cry out from pleasure because

it really doesn't hurt

at all

I just want you to keep

dipping your pen

in my ink

and writing your name on my wall. . .

My shadow's name is. . .

STAND STILL

Time is moving swiftly against the waves of the ocean

Where the moon controls how silently the waters crash

Alongside the sands beneath my feet where I walk

To the beat of your pounding heart

Inside

My mind where you rest for a moment just to breathe

The sound of my name in my inner ear

I

Stand still

just to hear your voice in the wind.

My hands to your hands,

my palms to your palms

My heart with your heart

I still stand without a

Sound...

Listening to what could be

Music to my soul

With my back turned

I feel what you feel

Want what you want

Crave what you crave

Believe what you believe and in the end

I **stand still** for you. . .

Stacey Barlow

TAKE IT TO THE HEAD (Stop Running)

Row, row, row your boat

gently down the. . .

looking into a shaded mirror

where phase number 1 lies

to you starring you

right in the face

without a smirk

or a hint of clarity

you break camp

phase number 2 tells

u the truth among all

truths

U wear colors to show

your identity of where u belong

but you are still beautiful in

her eyes

then u turn around and take her

to court just because

u don't agree with her rules

then get out of her house!

if u can't handle that kind of love

take it to the head

then break camp

row, row, row your boat

gently down the stream. . .

when you keep whistling that

tune

it all becomes clearer now

dearer now. . .

take it to the head

as phase 3 got u bent

like a pretzel all

out of shape

when a fight broke out

and you didn't desire to

participate

which is good because u

didn't have the need to. . .

take it to the head

merrily, merrily,

phase 4 got u sitting

straight up at attention

because the government

got their hands in

everything

from politics,

young world, boys, girls, teenagers, churches,

did I forget to mention

nutrition?

right down to the calories

counted on their plates

to the shoes tied on

their feet

when will they get a break?

too much pressure is set

on the shoulders of young ones

but phase 5 wants them to be grown

in a young mind's brain

so they break camp once again

Merrily, merrily, life is but. . .

A simple nod of the head
to say
you agree with such nonsense as this
back to the drawing board
that's phase 6

So when it's time to slow
down and
you have no place to run
take it to the head
and break camp alone
life is but a dream. . .

Because when you wake up

you're grown

TASTES GREAT

I lick my lips as my mouth

waters for that sweet salty taste of you

I unravel the package where I find

two

of the most

delicious looking nuts

wrapped in

partial cups as I. . .

continue

to melt with

anticipation

awaiting the moment that

I

can

wrap

my

tongue around your

chocolate edges

being careful not to

bite into you

so soon

I swoon

and swore I wouldn't

lick the middle until

you melted some more

as if the chocolate

melted on my fingertips

I lick what's left on my index

back down to my thumb

and then I start

on the other one

the other piece of chocolate

with half nut inside

it's hard like the first

I close my eyes

to take in again that

sweet salty taste of you

being careful not

to

bite around your chocolate edges

too soon

I still swoon

at the way you make me

Stacey Barlow

want more of you

and the way you

let me take control of my

tongue as you melt

once again between my fingertips

as I let the chocolate

run

on my index

I lick and lick and lick and lick

until there is no more left

to taste

I crave you because

I know you taste better

and now that you are inside of me

we have become

two great tastes that **taste**

great together

THE ELEVATOR

Michael had caught the Red Eye into town just to spend some time with me. I couldn't believe after all these years; the day had finally come that I received the chance to spend the evening with the ever so popular Michael Sikes.

"Ummm what a man."

The only thing was that he was 10 years my senior but, everyone has their taste of honey. Why shouldn't I? It was 8:15 p.m. Thursday night and Michael's plane dropped right on time.

"You're rather antsy tonight," Michael said as we walked casually back to the car.

"What? I don't get a kiss?"

I stopped in my tracks to catch my breath because the man's voice could hypnotize a woman's panties off. And please don't let him sing. I kissed him with the thought of how it used to be. The kiss set off sparks like a fourth of July celebration. We were quiet on the way back to the hotel that I had reserved for the two of us. As temperature rose, we couldn't wait to get inside. It was a good thing that I had given the bellhop an extra set of keys to fix up the place because I had no time to decorate. We spoke to the attending clerk, giggling like two teenagers at their prom. As we waited for the elevator to reach the first floor, Michael held me tightly and told me that he had been waiting forever until the day he could see me again. I searched his eyes for the truth. They never lied.

The elevator door opened and Michael held the door for me to step inside. I smiled politely. After the door shut, Michael grabbed me and put his mouth to mine. I couldn't breathe. What was this man doing?

"I need you now," he said in a panic.

"You'll have me as soon as we get to the. . ." he stopped me cold by placing his finger against my bottom lip.

He traced his tongue down the side of my neck as he proceeded to unbutton my blouse. He lifted my skirt to put his hands on my thighs. His hands were hot.

"Ummm easy access," he quipped.

I wrapped my arm around his neck, inviting him to partake of the madness that was stirring in me. With my back against the wall, he pressed the button to stop the elevator between floors.

"I know you want this. I know you want me," he said as he continued to pop every button that I had on my garments.

"Fuck you, you want me to want you," I responded back in a teasing manner.

"That's what I want you to do, fuck me." I was appalled at first but gave way to his demands.

I stroked him gently with his already erect penis, as he slid inside to feel me up with years of what he had held for me. Thrusting deeper, harder, and faster; it seemed like there was no time to waste. The motion slowed for a moment just to speed up again.

"I only want what you want to give me, and only me."

He whispered in a raspy voice. Once, twice, and the third time, Michael came.

He pulled out slowly so that I could feel every inch that had been inside me. Michael kissed me and fondled me until our breathing slowed. We looked at each other and laughed.

Too bad Michael didn't get to see the room.

TICK TICK BOOM (WOOSAAAAH Moment)

I laid into him like a mattress

And grilled him like cheese

"oh please baby baby please"

I suggest that you understand

My wants and my needs

To fulfill my every fantasy that she was given to me

WOOOOSAAAH

I was going to tell you eventually

Eventually?

So you're saying that if I hadn't asked you wouldn't

Have told me about your dirty deed

And hoping you can come back to me

And fill me with your nasty greed

And think that everything would be fine between you and me

WOOOOSAAAH

You got me twisted Shrek

And then had the audacity to say you

Didn't want to get her upset

What the heck?!

A complete stranger at that

What were you thinking?

WOOOOSAAAH

You had me fooled I must admit

Telling me one thing

I hope she was worth it

Worth my time

My energy

My heart

And my spirit

It's funny though

So I'll say it again

You had me fooled I must admit

Telling me one thing

WOOOOSAAAH

I sure hope she was worth it.

You jeopardized a friendship

For an uncommon piece

A total stranger at that

OH PLEASE!!!!!

I laid into him like a mattress

And grilled him like cheese

Then he called because of a guilty conscience

To try to put his mind at ease

WOOOOSAAAH

The last thing I said just to let him know

You cannot be trusted

So I'm letting you go

WOOOOSAAAH

TWIN FLAMES

The universe whispered to you loudly enough

Where you could hear it speak

but, did you listen?

I heard it in the middle of the night

as it

Came into my dreams and stepped to me

As boldly as I could

Hear your voice

And feel your

Breath on the

Back of my neck

That made my hair stand up

The universe gave me a chill

And spoke in a language

That only you could understand

And I was able to translate

My soul nature

My soul fire

My soul imagination of

the coolness that

Would not put out the heat

In a time where the universe

Heard my plea of

Desire and the desire

Is within me

And my soul stem reached you

As I reached out

To feel what the

Whisper was that you heard

But did you listen?

Days pass and I heard you tell the universe

The answer to the question it asks

Wait. . .

I was afraid to touch the **flame**

That only burned for you

Just because

The flame was meant for me

And it didn't burn

It only ignited

What was there all along

I touched the flame that only burned

For you

But did you listen to the universe?

I heard you

I felt you

I birth you

I melt you

But, did you listen?

WHO (Else) IS LOVING YOU?

I've walked around with a

Chip

On my shoulder

For the past two months

Wonder

If it was really Memorex

Or

It being over

We've played the game of tagged

On far better terms of

Whose it belong

To

With half a brain on standby

Thinking

Who (else) is loving you?

Tired of the bit by bit

Conversations

That give me pleasure only half the

Time

The other half is spent hoping

To be in your arms

Wanting to make you mine

Am I yours?

I will implore

Am I yours?

Please don't ignore

My simple cry to be closer

In your eyes

Your simple divine queen

To your rib

I know that I belong to you

Too

But in the back of my mind

I wonder

Who (else) is loving you?

I want to breathe your skin so

Deep that it feels like

You're inside of

Me

Where my inside will explode

With the fire of

Ecstasy

Please take my hand

And let me hold it

For

A lifetime of dreams

And in those dreams

I want forever

It

To be

Just you and me

I just want to know if

I can have you for

MY lifetime

And your moment

That will give you

More than just hours

I want to bring to you

That life and love

Beyond the sky

With all powers

From the South, North

West to East

I desire with all my heart

To have me you

So that our love lines

Will increase

Your ever whimper

Your every tear

My every solace

My every year

Your every touch

My every look

Your every sentimental

Value

Upon a water's

Brook

My ever patient being

My ever-quiet stands

Your every bit of enclosed anger

Your ever soft and tender hands

All I want is to be your rib

And make you happy a time or two

Stacey Barlow

I want to be your woman

And you to be my man

But first things first

Get my mind to stop wondering

Who (else) is loving you?

WHOLEHEARTEDLY (Reaching Out)

I want to put the past behind me

so that my present leads to my future

with only ME and YOU

we need to spend that

time together just

us

two

I want to put the past behind me so that my present leads to

my future with only YOU and ME with a love so strong

that only the angels

can see

I want to put the past behind me

so that my present leads to my future

with only YOU and I

I want it so far in the

past

that the tears I shed

rolling down my face

completely dries

I want to put the past behind me

so that my present leads to my future

with only I and YOU

we definitely need

to spend that time together

just

us two

I want to put the past behind me

so that my present leads to my future

with only WE

forsaking all

others

and building a stronger love

wholeheartedly

HEAVEN DOESN'T HAVE TO WAIT

Where did the time go

When there is nothing more that could be done

She sits on the bed

Left side knife ~ right side gun

Pointed to her head

She begged and pleaded for a

Second chance

To state her case with the

Demon inside her

Now she face

When there is nothing else to be done

This time

Right side knife ~ left side gun

She lays back wallowing in her tears

Looking up toward the ceiling asking God

To save her years

From torment

Lies,

Abuse

Neglect

Abandonment

Forgetfulness...

She closed her eyes in hope to see

A light

Once again she awakens to knife of the left~

Gun on the right

And sat up and in her hands she holds

What the future told

Of her existence

On a sheet of paper

It reads:

"The Lord Is My Shepard I shall NOT want He maketh me to lie down in green pastures: He Leadeth me beside the still waters" And she

stopped...

Knowing that waters run deep and she keeps reminding that her soul is safe with Him but, if

She did this she will not

Be forgiven

The paper still read:

"Yea tho I walk through the valley of the

shadow of death

I will fear no evil for Thou

Art with me Thy rod and Thy staff

They comfort me"

So she contemplated when there was

Only one thing left to be done

Drop the knife

And throw away the gun

So in the end she wouldn't have to say

Heaven doesn't have to wait.

ABOUT THE AUTHOR

A native of Hooks, Texas, Stacey continues write until her heart is content. She plans on traveling the world and spreading her love through the art of poetry. Stacey has appeared on several BlogTalkRadio shows which includes Virtikal Bistro, Vertikal Café, Poetically Spoken, Cyphers Den and hopes to continue to appear on more shows. She has also made an appearance at The Naked Bean Café in Shreveport, Louisiana 2008. Featured in Poetry And Prose magazine and contributes her writing skills to Jennings Wire and Elation Magazine. Recently became one of the contributing authors and #1 best-selling author, for the #1 best-seller "How Big Can You Dream?" Journal With International Authors To Make Your Dreams Come True," and contributed to "Poets of northeast Texas" by Nattyboyblac, Nathaniel Little.

www.ingramcontent.com/pod-product-compliance
Lightning Source LLC
Chambersburg PA
CBHW030614110526
44587CB00049B/373